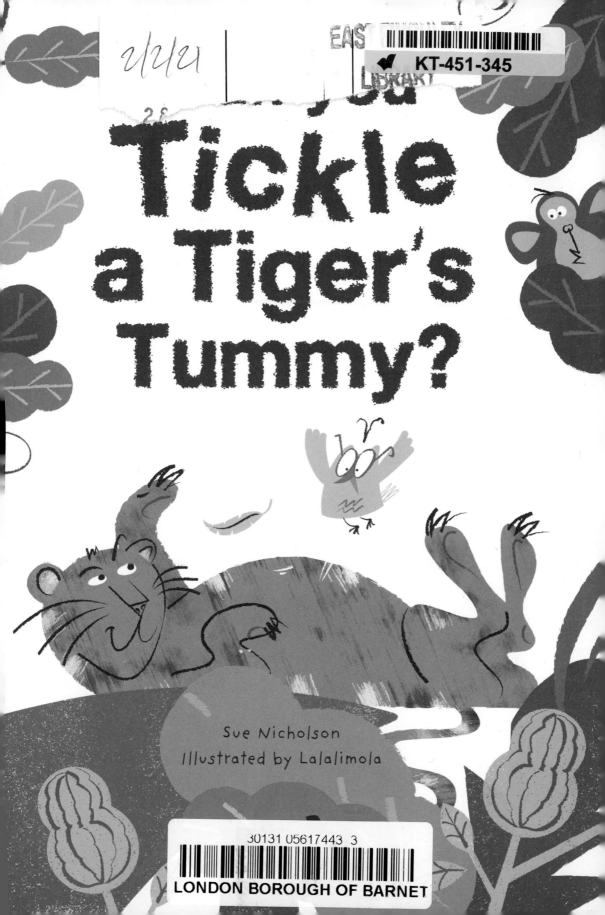

Tickle a Tiger's Tummy?

Sue Nicholson

Illustrated by Lalalimola

Can I run faster than a sloth?

Yes! The three-toed sloth is such a slowcoach it can take a whole minute to move just **four metres** (that's about ten steps)!

Because the sloth hardly moves, tiny green plants called **algae** grow in its fur.

The sloth only climbs down from its tree **once a week** to have a **poo!**

Why did the sloth sit on a clock?

To be on time!

Hundreds of beetles and moths live in the sloth's fur, feeding on the algae and other insects.

Can you **spot** the **know-it-all owl** and **owlets** as you read this book?

Can dogs talk?

Dogs bark, howl, growl, whimper and whine.
They may be saying **Play with me!**
Danger! Hello! or **Here I am!**

Dogs talk in other ways, too...

by **sniffing** each other's bottoms,

Hello, how are you?

by **wagging** their tails,

Play with me!

...or peeing on a tree or post to leave a **scent mark** for another dog to find.

Can you tickle a tiger's tummy?

A tiger may look **cuddly** like your pet cat, but it's **not** a good idea to tickle its tummy!

A tiger is a powerful **predator.** It kills by sneaking up on its **prey** and biting the back of their neck with its **10 cm-long** teeth. Yikes!

Tigers are wild animals and can be **dangerous.** Some tigers kill people who get too close to them.

But tigers are not fierce all the time. Just like pet cats, they like to:

Sleeeeeeeep,

lick their fur clean,

and... pounce!

Do fish have fingers?

No! But they have **fins**, which they move a bit like fingers.

Fish use their fins to help them **steer,**

balance in the
water and...

STOP!

There are about **30,000** kinds of fish.
Some can do **amazing** things with their fins.

Flying fish use their fins to **glide** through the air.

Frogfish use their fins to **crawl** across the seabed.

What's the stinkiest animal?

The skunk would win in the World's Most Stinky Animal competition. What a **WHIFF!**

If a skunk gets scared, it squirts a jet of stinky liquid out of its bottom, which smells **worse** than **rotten eggs.**

If that's not bad enough, the smelly liquid gets in your throat and makes your eyes water so you can't see, which gives the skunk time to run away!

Other animals use stinky smells
to protect themselves, too...

The **bombardier
beetle** squirts a
hot, smelly liquid
from its tummy.

The fluffy **fulmar
chick** vomits a
sticky orange goo
that stinks of
rotten fish.

Why do penguins waddle?

Penguins waddle because they have **short legs** and **long bodies,** so they sway from side to side when they're walking.

Even though they're birds, penguins cannot fly but they can....

slide...

Do snakes poo?

Many snakes **don't poo much** because they only eat a few times a year. Some can go without pooing for over a year!

Snake poo often has fur, teeth, nails and bones in it!

A giant snake can eat a whole antelope in one go!

All animals poo to get rid of waste food they can't use...

Elephants are big and eat a lot, so they make **HUGE** piles of poo every day.

Birds need to be light to fly, so they poo up to **50 times** a day, to get rid of waste food.

Dung beetles love poo. Some roll the poo into balls, then eat it or lay their eggs in it. Yuck!

Why do bees buzz?

On a warm summer's day you may hear **buzzing** as bees fly from flower to flower collecting pollen.

buzzZZZ

The buzzing is the sound of the bees' wings beating **super-fast** — around 230 times a second!

Bees beat their wings fast to help them **fly** and **hover** over flowers.

Bees sometimes buzz and do a little dance to tell other bees where to find the best pollen.

buzzzz

buzzzz

Some bees buzz to shake the pollen off the flowers so they can collect it more easily.

Say this ten times as fast as you can, without getting in a muddle...

Be a fizzy, fuzzy, buzzy, busy bee.

Do orangutans sleep in beds?

Yes, orangutans do sleep in beds, but not in beds like ours. They build themselves beds in **trees.**

Orangutans weave **BIG, bendy branches** into a base, then fill it with lots of leafy branches to make a **comfy mattress.**

Sometimes they add a leafy 'blanket', and a soft leafy 'pillow', too.

An orangutan usually makes a new leafy 'bed' **every day.**

Some orangutan beds have an extra 'mattress' on top, like a **bunk bed!**

Can ants sing?

Yes, but their songs aren't like the songs we sing.

We can't hear them, but ants can make **drumming, squeeeeeeaking,**

Ants make beautiful **music** by **rubbing** parts of their bodies together.

Sing to the ants...
Drag a comb over the edge of a ruler to make some ant sounds.

What's the biggest **ant** in the world?

An elephant!

rattling and scraping sounds.

Leafcutter ants make **sounds** when they are cutting leaves. This tells other ants to **help** them carry the leaves back to their nest.

Why do elephants have such BIG ears?

swish swish

To help them keep **cool**! Flapping their big ears makes a breeze — a bit like swishing a giant fan.

Elephants' big ears are good for other things, too...

Elephants have **amazing** hearing and can hear other elephants from over 10 km away — that's as far as about 100 football pitches!

They fan out their enormous ears to **SCARE** other animals away.

Can animals see me in the dark?

Some can! Many animals that come out at night have **BIG eyes** to help them see in the dark.

Animals that are busy at night are called **nocturnal** animals.

The tarsier's **GIANT** eyes help it to spot a meal in the dark, such as a tasty insect or a scrummy lizard.

Bats 'see' in the dark by **squeeeeeaking.**

Squeak! Squeak!

Squeak!

The squeaks bounce back from things, which tell the bats where those things are.

Owls can see well in the dark, too. They have **HUGE** eyes for the size of their heads.

Do sharks brush their teeth?

Sharks **don't** brush their teeth with a toothbrush and toothpaste. But they open their mouths so tiny **cleaning fish** can swim inside and nibble away bits of food.

Yum!

Even though sharks eat fish, they don't eat the busy, cleaning fish because they are doing a useful job.

Crocodiles don't brush their teeth, either.

Crocs let little birds hop inside their mouths to peck out bits of rotten food. That way, the crocs get clean teeth and the birds get a tasty meal!

What did the shark eat after he'd had his teeth checked?

The dentist!

Can frogs fly?

Yes! If it's in danger or spots a tasty snack on another tree, a tree frog **leaps off** a branch, **spreads out** its big webbed feet and **glides** through the air.

The stretchy skin on the tree frog's feet slows it down as it flies through the air — a bit like using a parachute.

The **squishy, sticky** pads under the tree frog's toes help it to make a soft landing and 'stick' to a tree trunk, so it doesn't fall off.

Frogs that live on the ground can't fly. They get around by **swimming** and **hopping** instead!

Can animals build houses?

Yes, some animals can build amazing homes — they just don't look like the kind of homes we build.

Termites are **master builders**. Their nests look like **tall chimneys** and are home to **thousands** of tiny termites.

Home Sweet Home

Beavers **build** dome-shaped lodges out of branches and mud.

Meerkats **dig** underground homes with lots of tunnels and rooms.

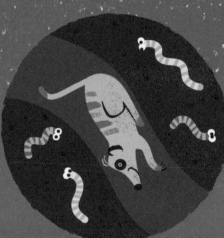

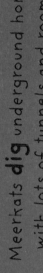

Weaver birds **weave** grass into hanging nests.

Why are ladybirds spotty?

Ladybirds' spots **warn** other animals that they **don't taste good** to eat.

Ladybirds can be bright **orange, red** or **yellow** with black spots.

The record number of spots for a ladybird is **24**! Have you ever seen a 24-spotted ladybird?

Other animals have **warning colours**, too.

This blue-ringed octopus has rings on its body that flash **electric blue**.

This poison dart frog is bright **golden yellow**.

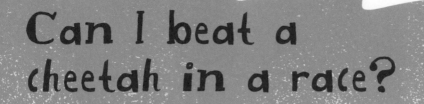

Can I beat a cheetah in a race?

ostrich

pronghorn antelope

No cheating!

gazelle

hare

No, a cheetah can run as fast as **120 km** an hour. That's **three times _faster_** than the fastest person on the planet!

The cheetah can only run really fast in short bursts, though, such as when it's chasing a tasty antelope. Then it has to have a rest.

Here are some of the fastest animals on land:

What's a cheetah's favourite food?

Fast food!

kangaroo

cheetah

Which end of a worm is which?

I'm your tail, silly!

Hello, who are you?

It's hard to tell which end of a wriggly, wiggly worm is which because **both ends** look the **same**...

...but look closer and you'll see a **thick band** near one end. The worm's head is at the end nearest this band. The other end is its bottom.

Do birds use umbrellas?

Some birds use leaves as **mini umbrellas** to shelter from **heavy rain** and keep their feathers **dry.**

If birds' feathers get too wet, it's hard for them to fly.

Other birds love getting wet. Swans make a kind of oil, which they rub through their feathers to keep them **waterproof.**

Even though many birds shelter from heavy rain, they still like to **SPLASH** in a bath, to clean their feathers!

How does a spider catch its dinner?

Many spiders spin webs to trap insects for their dinner. They make their webs with **strong, sticky** spider silk.

The spider wraps a trapped insect in silk thread so it can't get away. Then it poisons the insect to turn it into a **slurpy soup.**

Orb spider webs are round, like **wheels.** Other webs are shaped like **baskets, funnels or sheets.**

It can take a spider **an hour** to spin a new web.

Do animals play hide and seek?

Yes, many animals hide so other animals can't find them. **Stick insects** hide from hungry birds and lizards by looking like **twigs** or **leaves!**

Can you spot four stick insects hiding on this tree?

Some stick insects are **brown**, like branches. Some are **green**, like leaves.

If it's in real danger, a stick insect drops to the ground and pretends to be **dead!**

Other animals **hide** to catch their prey.

Can you spot the flower mantis insect camouflaged as a flower?

Some stick insects sway so they look like little twigs swaying in the breeze.

Which animals are like rainbows?

Rainbowfish get their name because they're all the colours of a rainbow.

Rainbowfish aren't born with their **beautiful** colours. They get more colourful as they grow older.

Here are some other brightly
coloured creatures:

This **toucan's** jazzy beak scares
away predators and helps it to
spot a mate in the forest.

This **roller's** bright
colours help it to
attract a mate.

The flashy colours of this
rainbow grasshopper warn
other animals to stay away.

This **chameleon's**
brilliant colours show
how it feels.

Which animal is a sleepyhead?

The sleepy **dormouse** curls up in a **warm, cosy** nest when it gets cold, and only wakes up when the weather is warm again.

Going into a deep sleep like this is called **hibernating.**

The dormouse can sleep for up to **seven months** a year. What a sleepyhead!

grrr!

Bears are sleepyheads, too!
Bears sleep a lot during winter
but they don't go into a deep
sleep and can wake up very
quickly if they're disturbed...

...so never walk past
a sleeping bear!

THINGS to MAKE and DO

Pet-watching
If you have a pet cat or dog, watch how it moves and plays, hunts or says 'hello'. Talk to your child about how many of the things it does are similar to its relatives living in the wild.

Make a cardboard creature
Save cardboard tubes and turn them into colourful cardboard creatures. Paint with thick poster paint, then glue on eyes, ears and feet. Draw on features with a black felt-tip pen.

Be a bee or a frog
Pretend to be one of the animals you have read about in this book. Can you buzz like a bee, race like a cheetah or hop like a frog?

Visit a zoo
Visit a zoo, wildlife park or an aquarium to find out about the different kinds of wonderful animals that share our world.

Quarto Knows

Quarto is the authority on a wide range of topics.
Quarto educates, entertains and enriches the lives of our readers—enthusiasts and lovers of hands-on living.
www.quartoknows.com

FSC www.fsc.org
MIX
Paper from responsible sources
FSC® C104723

© Quarto Publishing plc
Illustrations © Sandra Navarro/Lalalimola 2017
First published in 2017 by QED Publishing
an imprint of The Quarto Group.
The Old Brewery, 6 Blundell Street, London,
N7 9BH, United Kingdom.
T (0)20 7700 6700 F (0)20 7700 8066
www.QuartoKnows.com

A catalogue record for this book is available from the British Library.

ISBN 978 1 78493 837 6

Author: Sue Nicholson
Editors: Carly Madden and Catherine Veitch
Designer: Victoria Kimonidou

Manufactured in Dongguan, China TL122017
10 9 8 7 6 5 4 3 2 1